A WATER CYCLE

A WATER CYCLE

Poems by Eleanor Keats

*A passage through life, with
beginnings, middles, ends, and
meditations that float between
and around: to be read as one poem.*

DAWN VALLEY PRESS
New Wilmington   Pennsylvania

A WATER CYCLE

Printed in the United States of America
First Printing

Library of Congress Catalog Card Number 85-073376
ISBN 0-936014-16-4

Front cover and inside artwork by Gigi Keats

This publication is supported by a grant from the Commonwealth of
Pennsylvania Council on the Arts.

Dawn Valley Press
Box 58
New Wilmington, PA 16142

ACKNOWLEDGEMENTS

"The Turtle" originally appeared in *The Antioch Review*, Vol. 19, No. 3 (Fall, 1959); Copyright 1959 by *The Antioch Review*. "They promenade along the beach," "Two people in a boat," and "Rain Forest with Children" originally appeared in *The Bloomsbury Review*. "Wet jaggedness" appeared in *The Cornell Review*. "Solitary" and "Nature, you weather me wrong" appeared in *St. Andrews Review*. "Rain on the Lake," "And is the light of the sea," "If I face the breakers," and "Upon Looking at a Wilson Cloud-Chamber Photograph" first appeared in *Sunrust*. "And as their ancestors had done" was published in the *Religious Humanist*. "And I was born on that day of the big explosion" first appeared in the Ohio Arts Council Anthology, *Good Old Poems I Love Them*. "Songs for Jeremy" first appeared in *Touching This Earth*, an anthology of fourteen women poets. "Children" first appeared in *Spree*. "Mr. Batdorf" first appeared in *Sojourner*.

With deep gratitude to the Pennsylvania Council on the Arts for a generous grant, and to the other kind patrons of the arts whose support helped make this book possible.

To Don, Gigi, Jeffrey and Jocy

CONTENTS

Who is waiting
inside in the room
with the rain
as sharp as swords on the roof,
with the rain
as thick as swords on the fields,
as wide as drums on the world?

(Who is hiding
enclosed in the womb
with the warmth inside
and the fright around
strange sounds around
in the wide dark world
strange fears in the dark wide world?)

Oh, man is hiding
snug and small,
so wound to life
and bound to fall,
so wound and bound
as the sun and the moon
before the dark end of the world.

PART I

PART I

NET FISHING: ILE D'OLERON

At night, you spread the silent nets.
Fish, blind in the dark, rush forward
without sound, slip into the mesh
of your trap, slim bird bones
of winged fins catching like hooks
in the tentacles of your knots.
You sport, like any other
fisherman in the dusk,
the sun dropping red. When the catch
is done, in the morning, you raise
the radiant grill of your nets from water,
counting the slim, iridescently silver
bodies, part fish, part evolving bird
in the spread of tail and fin.
Then hang the translucent grid
between trees, and unpeel the caught bones,
unhinge the open mouths, still sucking air

Who remembers that feeling
of climbing over the last high con-
cealing dunes, only to be stunned
in the ears by the furious sound,
socked in the lungs by the enormous
draft of air shot over the long sea
by the waves, with such force, the lungs balloon
up and the throat hurls out seagull cries,
the feet already lifting from the ground,
the soul already vaulting into the open space,
freed from the cities of manmade and the down-
drafts caught in the smog between buildings,

        catapulting
        into the air
        of spume and seagull,

        a white beginning
        and a white ending
        in full circle,

        the curve of the wave
        upward with verve,
        the pulling back
        of the cycle,

        then in cataclysms breaking,
        into joy,
        into sorrow,

             all,
    white   effervescence,
             all,
white water   white wings

You were born here:
in a burst of atoms,
in a spray of fervor,
coming over the earth's edge
where eveything is molten fire,
malleable clay, pulsating,
washed clean again and again
by the ocean's sides,
by the clattering sieve
of the moon's tides.

Who knows
what new combinings
will be caught here:
a something
shining with radiance,
found only in the baptism of water
and the purifying of the bath,
in the amorphous flow of the earth's skin,
in light's cosmic prism
and in sound's miraculous ear,
undulating in waves,
refracting,
forever new,
minute by minute,
whatever can be born
of body or thought.
Life begins here.

You begin by floating in the ocean,
a bobbing cork, a flick of jetsam,
almost pure liquid
in the broad limpid sweep,
darkened in shadow
by the occasional swoop
of a gull's wing, almost
a scrap for his searching,
yet he prefers fish.

You merge with water,
floating outside
the houses perched-on-cliffs
that might be your home.
They are nothingness
when you drift
like wood in water,
looking out from space
towards the specks of cozy fire
that might be inside that place;
out here, the vista is too wide
and the substance too liquid
for four square walls of thickness.

Do not lose this scope.
It will tide one over
in the bad times ahead.
You and the sea
are one undefined and soft beginning.
Your importance is nil,
though still, everything is possible.
You are a drop of the world.

You go from a long sleep
to a still longer sleep,
pulsing out your living and dying
in a flow of sighing and panting,
a rising fall that continues forever in tides,
a sleep that merges in seas,
an animal breathing
from an animal's core,
uninhibited and soft like a cat,
heavy with lust like a panther,
blackly lapping
on the shores of our unconscious
mirages blooming out of dust
or suicides in cleft canyons.
We grow and rest
and grow again,
a rhythm almost knocked out of us
in cities, where the frenetic beat
jangles our breathing
until it gets caught in our chests,
until our bellies find it again
only when we sleep,
on the edge of seas,
on the edge of the universe.

Our tides are war,
        and peace,
our tides are moons
        to conquer, and shores
            to make tidy,
our tides are loves,
        and labors,
            and procreations,
        are heaving women,
            and wailing newborns,

our tides are lives in the harness
          of fate, which we partly make
and partly take, in its
          concatenation of events and place,
until there finally comes
          that last oblivion
when the rhythm of the universe
          plays our tune upon its catguts
to the strumming end of time
          and space.

They promenande along the beach.
An opening explodes in their lungs.
The cities are spewing out of the abyss.

Somewhere else,
far into nothingness,
a man and woman sit
under an orange and green umbrella.
They are gazing into a sea of eyes
and into the long wave
unrolling along the edge of their bodies.

A white gull bursts
from the white surf.
The wind whirls wing
and water together
until I can't tell
earth from air,
fire from substance.

Everyone else has gone home,
leaving the beach the way it was
when rock was pulverized into sand.

Light strikes from above

the bodies that move along the beach
are drowned in light

the waves glow from within,
unroll the message of their scrolls
again and again,
exploding into light
as they explode into sound

until we find the exit from our bodies,
walk over the wind-flattened sea
like Moses answering Jehovah,

climb rungs of light
hanging from the clouds,
communicate,
between sky and water

expand further over the open sea,
catching the high currents of air,
then shrieking in our dive downwards,
over the catapulting of waves,
over the frenzy of the foam:
"free me, free me",

and as we splinter
outwards and upwards,

forget we ever had bodies
nailing us to one moment
or to one place

forget the dialogue
of corruption

the sound
of the gun-packed air

the cymbal-clash
of money

step just once
into the light

and become pure being

∽

Moss and butterflies
cocooned me
by dappled streams,
the shiny prisms of dew
shimmering
in the damp shade
of green canopies.

Trout flicked up
like silver lights,
and every dream
smiled glinting
on the shining patches
of water, and on the rays,
filtering through
the forests of the sky.

Those images haunt me now,
in my city sleep,
winding around
my heavier feet
like roots around
boulders; light
and shadow bend
more to the shadow
in unbalanced weight,
with cares dragging
my shoulders down
and mosses killed
by my heavier tread.

Now all the days ahead
will close in dreams
about that brook,
about the golden-bursting feel

within the private solitude:
to live, without constraint,
to glimmer after things
and keep the feelings secretly
tucked down in pockets,
beside jewel rocks,
birds' feathers,
butterflies' wings,
beside gnarled roots
and pocket knives
asserting our lives.

FATHER POEM

Father, you shrink me
box within smaller box
till my last square
breath of will
caves in,
deader
than that count-down
silence
that engulfed
our first father-daughter
tête à tête
at the corner place.
It would have been an occasion.
But you kept ramrod still
by your plate,
unable to ask or stir
anything.
The liquid in my glass
froze in my throat
as the bomb arose towards
my heart and blasted it out
completely.
We were worse than strangers.
We had lived in the same house
for decades,
yet had not the slightest key
to each other.
I knew how childhood could be
from those first-year photos
in the attic,
springing from your square carriages
with devil in my eyes.
But you arrested that.
I would have been liquid,

with clay for fists
and paint for fingers,
dripping over your well-kept lawns
in the spray of turned-on hoses;
but you always came
and turned them off.
I could have grown
through pavements, then,
but you plucked me.
Now all the other
silent children
are tearing apart
the molds
their silent fathers
set them in.

MOTHER POEM

Dropped your hands
on the piano keys
with the rebound
of a spring,
the weight of your arms
hammer blows
throbbing
the force
the force
of your beaten spirit

the climaxes unresolved
the flight into arpeggios
the lift, the lift
of total escape
ripples, cascades, spent journeys!

heavy arms,
flung in despair,
beating fingers,
restless!
the falling down
the rising up
you, mother mother
the angel I hid under

like under the wing
of the piano,
under its vibrations,
absorbing your unhinged soul

it poured into me
the anguish, the terror, the search
the unresolved climaxes

through the wires
of the piano,
pounding on me
electrically,
charging me up
to excess,

and now,
my only escape . . .
into
the dissolution
of
song

I   cast   my   wards,   pails   hanging
                  past   like
                  back-   two

from my   shoulders'   ther,   rails   I
                  yoke,   fa-
                  mo-   ther,

cannot carry   any   split   er   pairs.
                  further,   in
                  nor   light-

I spill   both   and   are   too
                  waters in;   o-
                  lakes   ceans

small to   sweep   bur-   they   never
                  away   den,
                  the   weights

meant to   lay   my   yet   stern
                  u-   back,
                  pon   and

words of   lov-   upset   esteem,   stealing
                  ing   the
                  can   self-

the days   of   away   hidden   stream
                  joyous   from
                  quest   that

of jeweled   moss,   to   I   pour,
               respond-   the
               ing   step.

therefore,
     like   some   liba-   rificing   all
               un-   tion,
               holy   sac-

the quiet   trust   for   into   brooks,
               they   me,
               felt   pour

streams, lakes and   forty   forty   nights,
               o-   days
               ceans,   and

the backward   flood-   my   rest   in
               ing   soul,
               of   then

fear, but   feel   is   securely   blessed.
               my   at
               oneness   last

We thought we were safe
in the ocean of our parents,
but oceans shrank to rivers
narrowing through rocks
and now my sliding steps
are turning downward,
following the cutaway path
from security to shock,
my senses squeezing out
another path to the same yearning,
that oneness youth must
tear out from its source;

now a new being, unenveloped
by the egg, is feeling its shaking
feet and force.

What deep crevices to go through,
searching for my reflection.
The dark gorge-pools
are dank, mysterious mirrors
that send my reflection back
so violently,
I dare not look or drink:
I become dark satyr,
evil Poseidon;
I stand electric and exposed,
a disconnected wire,
burning to be enveloped again.

But my path is cut off;
the bridge has crumbled under.
I must follow the way
that the waters squeeze out,
through doubtful turns,
anxieties at the slippery edge

of new corners, new ways
beckoning at untried crossroads,
or risky downslides in my daze.

It is damp and fecund here,
and life abounds in micro-
scopic algae and cells.
Yet I feel, at times, there is
no other living thing.
At other moments,
profound as rock,
my senses plummet
in the gorge-cut wells,
black as Italian pools
stark with cypress.
Nursing in their darkness,
like some weird changeling,
until I feel immersed in full
and strangely baptized,
I emerge again,
no longer novice to myself,
but seeking a new sanctuary.

The black-green waters
surge forward now,
doubling up and gathering force;
the widening surge increases
as light flickers up ahead,
bubbling along a broader course
until converging currents
blast the rocks like thunder,
a wetness exiting with exultations,
a bursting swell of waterfall
jubilant over rocks
in cascades of sheet silver.
I am born again
on its bubbling.

THE GORGE

Wet jaggedness scrapes the rocks round
Piling fume white-high, and sound and sound:
Roars and subsides, then roars again,
Force, fleet shadows plummet, resounding! when
Up, over, all, splashes, scrapes, cascades, crashes:
The gorge-rock rounds barely under grey-green
                    whip-lashes

A bird each one hundred years picks up a grain
                    from the sand of the sea
The length of this task gives him rest once he
                    reaches eternity

Sift through the foam, strike the rock
Bruise your wings through the wet beauty — shock,
Foil soul with treacherous moss, soft with slime,
Soak, soak and soak past mortal time

You were waiting for me,
under the mirror shine,
my completion, my other self,
the water into which I pour myself;
your image had always been fleeting,
but so recognizable when it came
in greeting. Like so many other things,
I should have known I would
lose you through drowning.
Is that why our gaze
had a slight mien of frowning?

In the water's stir, your mouth
talked back to mine; your eyes flowed
muted in response. In the ripples
of the lake, you gathered close to me
and we swam together as two swans,
following the quiet circles of
our dance; only later
to make our first mistake.

It was chance that we looked
into the same lake at the same time.
It was chance again
that you disappeared from view.
The matings that mate forever,
in time of strife and war,
are infinitely strong, yet
also infinitely few.

I watched you go down,
and my image also split asunder;
you bobbed up once, but it was
too late to save you. You soon
were washed away from me
by lightning forks and peals of
thunder; first near, then far,
by seconds, then by years;
first drowned by love,
then drowned by tears.

What smooth eddies you make,
o terrible swan,
along the mirror lake.
You echo song like shells,
kiss in awe the crook of your reflection
until you reach the shore,
stretch your soft fool-feather wings so vast
above your hard male-muscled legs,
do not sing, alas,
but squint your beady eyes
that out of water hide so treacherously small
in what seems an outstretched fist,
and with your tight, hard thighs,
o swan, my swan,
no longer still, no longer shy,
but with a reptile's hiss,
you shatter all heaven for me
as you shake out your disguise.

THE TURTLE

Who, even in his most divine image,
does not feel with you the sudden desire
to bury all within oneself;
nor feel alike so encased and low,
so heavy to drag about in the open day;

Even in his most perpendicular, who is not drawn
to the cold, still rough inchoate form
of all crawling things, so like the child
before he has the strength to stand,
so like the man, in his soul's dragging depths!

Yet, after such low crawlings,
(looking even like an infant in your gentler gazes),
when you suddenly find a morsel for your hunger:

Your eyes glint hard, you arch your neck,
Your jaw drops wide,
And I lose you to that silent world inside.

I run to the refraining sea

Waves are hurling against the beach
It is twelve o'clock
Nobody is swimming to the other side
of the world

Waves are hurling against the beach
Bottles with messages
are hurtling onto the shore like dead fish
Too many people are calling, calling
for help

What sharp thrust,
crux of Cain,
pierces the heart of man
(this man),
bound to pain
and the crumbling dust.

Pitched to the pith,
can blood still pulse
from a torn heart,
from the broken and apart,
or must all convulse
while the thunders rain
to one pitch?

Yes!
Touched to our quick,
torrents in the brain
flood merciless upon its heights.
Only imagine, try, the frights:

Sights in images thick
and sounds fiercely sprung
towards unsung tones,
unChristian moans,

Inarticulate roars,
shattering to the bone,
and more insistent than the rain.

O dissonant madrigal,
fierce rushing fire,
the vibrating reeds of this boneful lyre
sing out the friction of love

Shadow engendering cloud,
rain tearing birth,
the sun-scorched crust of revolving earth
seeds the thirsting of love

Sea emptying wave,
dry rainbow sky,
your blinding look and your deafening cry
stun the heaven of love

Heart pealing gong,
dust crumbling bone,
the echoing cries of a tumbling stone
sound the bell of love

Pain shooting world,
I hang on your banging tone;
feeling my flesh kiss my crumbling bone
let me swing with the clang of love

Solitary,
inside bottles
lying side by side
on silent shelves:
under our corks,
filled to bursting,
yet, in our smooth
externals,
thirsting for a blending
rarely found;
we search
for liquifaction
in each other,
evaporation
into soul and air,
warm red bodies
flowing
in each others' spirits,
heady wines
that warm us
out of time,
out of our glass
strait-jackets
forever locking us up
from each other.

Prisoners hiding in pockets of cells,
hanging like bells in limbo: tolling
their tales locked in riddles, frantic, fathomless,
riddled from weapons and worms and words
piercing their skins; here cast on limbs outstretched
like slow-scorched salamanders glued to hot walis
or like butterflies' wings pinned flat paperwise;
racked as in sun, though, there, really in shadows so deep,
as if dropped through dank holes and drearily falling
(one by one) on each other, and clanking in chains;
though pain is felt less under water, and rain
cannot wet you once you are wet, and these
cells-locked-by-cells, over cells, under cells,
all untouching, are deep under water;
for nothing so dark can resurface
where light would expose it and no one accept it,
except other prisoners, riddled in still worse chambers,
become, once part human, both eyeless and toothless,
tunneling forward through bodies in limbo, dank
carcasses slaughtered in masses, their bells
no more tolling, for rust and frustration,
forgotten: where are they? their voices?
all drowned in dark waters, though someone could
hang them in sculpture, bang them outstretched
in still pockets, stretch them on arms of corroded
metal, and put them in courtyards
somewhere, near dripping water, where
no one would understand.

How blesséd you are
to have a blanket of snow
pulled up over your scars.

My covers do not stay
but a night, though in the deep
folds, my days
are slow to speak.

Blesséd is the land
that mends so quick
blessed by the snow
that falls so thick.

Nine black monks with candles
wind over the snow,
with night as their backdrop.
Time is lost in the dark
behind, and space is too wide
stretching soft below.
The crooked and straight are
softened with white.
Time and eternity are
lit up by light.

There are no faces under those hoods.
Your candle too is a journey with night,
a looking in on, a sharing,
a procession on snow,
a sharing of darkness with the light.

Drops of the world
falling
falling
in
linear
flight,
infinite
drops
irresistibly
drawn
to the
water
below,

frail
molecules
adding up
in
downward
drops
to our
destinies,

a
lost
vapor,
a
liquid
air

split
in
its
hitting
into
transience

what
do

at
first
one
drop
at
a
time
in
a
splashed
orbit,

a
light
rebounding
of
spreading
circles,

a
heavenly

centers
of
gravity
depressing
the
waters
under
each
fragile
mass

a
heavenly
giving
and
taking

hovering
in
air,
yet

always
pulled
steadily
down,

still,
though
moving,
finite,
yet
followed
always
by
more
drops

in
mathematical
curtains,
in
cosmic
ladders,
leading
down,
yet
leading
up

staccato
dropped
liquid
pebbles
echoing
out
in
rings
over
the
lake

a
stigmatic
touch
shot
down
in
arrows

splashing
each
in
its
cosmic
orbit

they
add
up
to,
those
fractured
clouds
dropped
in
fistfuls
of
pearls

merged
in their
splintered
fallings
into
bottomless
lakes,
into
responsive
but
faceless
fluids

never stopping
in their
steady
spotted
sheet
falling
all at once
over
the
lake
hung
in
abstract
time,
in
visual
dots
miniature
globules
of
refraction
equal
equations
exchanging lives

REFLECTIONS

      JADE   shad-   locked   shade
             ow-   under
             cells   water,

    length-   (sight
      en-   break-
      ing   ening),
      thought,   Wak-en-ing!

      time-   slum-   matter   feelings
      light   ber-   stretch-   mumbling
                 ing,   ing
                           down,

    Under the   shad-   links,
             ow-   o-
             links,   Sing to the   Bob   O

    Link-   mysteries,   links of the shadows,   Speak-
    ed

    ing together,   fath-   cell   leafy ge-
                                 oms   pockets,
                                 in
                                 har-   Bells,
                                 mo-
                                 ny,

    om-   hold-   each   up,   deep
    e-   ing   other   in
    tries,   the
                                    wa-
                                    ter,

    lum-   daughters   slow   re-
    i-   of   flec-
    nous   light,   tions,

Ride me   be-   surfaces,   slide   lo
              neath   shin-ing   me   do
                                      (hide
                                    me),

       Not lie till we (show me), O
                     die.

I am floating in a
        boat
The wind is blowing
            me
where it will
I am eating coffee cake
        and cold grapes
The oars have flown
        from my hands
The sun has become
            my face
I am dissolving
        into liquid gold
The lake has taken
            over,
    the edges of land
    have all drowned
White trees have turned into
    long tongues, lapping at me
Purple weeds have become
        fluttering tapestries,
            inviting me in
Green leaves are all holding
            green hands
        like geometric claspings
            of molecules
Willow trees float their
        restless harpstrings
    to the bottom of time
A clatter of geese land
            from nowhere
        on nothing palpable
I am at the disposal
            of the wind
My eyes are resting
    on the shiny backs
        of turtles

I have entered the cathedral
     of water
I have melted into gold
   and silver and green
I am waiting for rain
     to open the pores
        of my skin
I am no longer in charge
     of my body

WATERLILIES

1

the waterlily
    rose
and gave its hands
    up to light
and brushed the black
    mud
off its petals

2

out of twenty
waterlily pads
    springs
    only one
    white
    flower

3

there are as many
    dark green pads
    as there are
    people
choking the earth

4

if there weren't
    mud
there wouldn't be
    waterlilies

5

if you stand
    proud
    like the white
waterlily flower,
    the mud will
    slide
off your back

6

there is no greater
    coolness
than a drop of rain
    rolling off
the petal of a waterlily

7

even the flat
waterlily pads
    are useful,
frogs need somewhere
    to sit

8

i am still looking
    inside
the petals
    of the waterlily
    to find
the secret
    of being

9
in the flux of
    reflections
    in the pond,
nothing shines
    brighter
than the waterlily

10
you can go over a
    waterlily
a hundred times
with your boat
it will always
    spring
    back

11
in the mirror
   of the pond,
i meet my image
coming and going,
like the waterlily
sinking into forgetfulness

12
a naked child
with golden hair,
    a waterlily
    in a pond:
    two loves
with hidden stems

13
the willow
    splinters
into a universe
    of strings
    underwater,
but the waterlily shines
    complete

14
i can look inside
the waterlily's cup
from petal-opening
to petal-closing,
and never become
    old

15
why are water
and the waterlily
inextricably united?
is there any other flower
    baptised from birth?

16
the asian sits on top
of the lotus blossom
i get eaten by the petals
    of the waterlily

17
is there any light
    greater
than the reflections
in a waterlily pond?
are there any spaces
        deeper
than the darkness sinking
   under the waterlily?

18
not even all of China
     is so myriad
as a pond of waterlily pads

19
only fools
try to clear
waterlilies
from a pond

20
if i follow
reflections
to their end
around the edges of the waterlily
i will never return
from the underworld

21
if i break off a petal
from one side of the waterlily,
i grow tall;
if i break off a petal
from the other side,
i grow small;
you must eat it whole
    to become a god

22
who am i
to ask questions
   of waterlilies?
i am still following
the aura of reflections
to the bottomless hall
    of the pond

Riches   gather   of war
sadly   in a   and
                          swell   greed.
Whatever   is   coldly   possessed,
   filters   through   the   fingers
and   is   washed   away,
   along   with   ethics   and   love.
No possessions   are   ever   enough,
          nor   is   one   ever   freed
                          from them,

                    but   here,
                    at   5 o'clock,
                          see,
diamonds   are   dancing   on   the   lake,

          in   the   mirror   shine
                    of   water,
               riches   are   change;
          every   second   is   haloed
          with   light's   rearranging
               on lakes   and   bays,
     in   the   shining   back   of   rays.

     To   each   therefore   his   own   gathering
                          of riches.
               For   me   none   compare
          with   the   flaked-gold   ricocheting
               of   the   sinking   sun
dusted   out   in   its   hammered-thin   sheet   over   the
6 o'clock   lake,   so   shimmery   and   shiny,
          like   burnt-copper   dragonflies
          darting   about   its   taut   face,
          like   wild   treasure
showered   in   a   dazzle   to   be   raked   in.

The   vision   lies   a   bit,   of   course,
  for   rays   do   not   dart;   but   for   the
            sake   of   art,   we   let
            our   eyes   betray   us
                in   this   trance.
        Reflections   are   really   a   dance
  from   each   prismic   pocket   that   ripples   make,
drawing   their   lightshooting   patterns   in   alternate
    waves,   in   flickers,   as   the   waters   shake
gently   from   the   shore   air;   all   light
    reflected   there   is   deflected   back   high   again
            as   rays   and   water   interchange
                their   elemental   nature.
  I   am   no   seeker   of   pirate   treasure,
        but   rather   a   dark   creature
                whose   measure   is
                water   and   light,
    the   two   forever   lifting   me   high
        from   the   drowning   dark   of
                night.

The world spins, and invisible currents flash,
just as my mind's currents clash.
I am no less than the shock and spark
of the world's aether, for similar stuffs in the dark
create, fuse and unfold. We are all molded
from the same chain as the atom;
even the daily rain is forged
from the same fire; the chords and
discords of the lyre, from the same
atuning of sound's ragged waves.
Measure and form are merely a tether,
alike for disturbances of the spirit,
as for the thundering of the wave

The silent shapes have many a fury
within; in the gentle streams
many a furious life is spawned;
and all creation is done in quiet.
The shape of a tree is not the tree,
but all is flux and spin

How much exists that I cannot see?
How much is countless explosions spent,
the silent blowing up from life to death
in a space we cannot see
and a time we cannot bend

It is not the shapes men make,
shapes disclosing violent power
(great feats of little men),
but the shapes already made
that shout in the eternal blast
with their unending fury.
And I, small shock and spark, endure,
and bless the engendering fury too

∿

UPON LOOKING AT A WILSON CLOUD-CHAMBER
PHOTOGRAPH

Whoever called reality
treeshapes, sunglobes,
or running rivers,

lived before
we could afford to take
the crooked atom's shape
with any trace of seriousness,
before we saw the atom
split the earth in chains
and wreck my date of birth
into indelible nightmare,
but especially before
the probing scientists could catch
the trembling display of matter
with their radiographs of vibrant rays,

scintillations of unseeable geometries,
of lives and half-lives
in their tethered, shimmering lines,
and their chaotic, broken trails;

before we could witness
particle capturing particle,
or the last sad deflection of a bit of matter
by something smaller still
than the atom

And as their ancestors had done, they were doing,
those golden men squat in that tiny fishing boat
on the great globe's drop, sail to the wind

But the sail was suddenly sucked upward,
and the fish hung dead on their hooks,
ticking away the decay of time,
the burnt universe's order

And the unknowing sons of those ancestors lamented,
not that matter was suddenly disturbed, but only
that the golden fish no longer could be sold.
Only later did they feel the burn
of the new chaotic sun, of the fast and sudden
ticking away of time

And I was born
on that day of the big
explosion,
and I was born
on that day
when matter was violated by man,
and I was born
on that day
when God gave up the ghost
after seeing his child charging
at the reins of the sun chariot
when one hundred thousand bodies
whirled back into atoms
in just one second of seared flesh
and now we had eaten
the poisoned apple on the tree
and the earth would continue
to be poisoned
and the air would continue
to be impure,

And I was born
on that day
when my birthday
turned into a deathday,
even though the planet
still whirled around,
even though the skin
is not hanging from my flesh,
nor am I burned with napalm,
or branded with the star of David
like the children
of my ancestors
who were hurled into ovens
even as they wrote poems
about butterflies,
as I now write poems about death,
to atone for my birthday of death

Crab   crab   what cancer jolts me
out of my skin so violently,
I hermit in your shell.
Frustration turns me armor savage, and eats
away at my core. My ocean waters
bore me not only Venus-like and virgin
on a scallop shell, gold-tinted hair
blowing in a Godlike wind; no, pity!
they gathered war as well, and now they harvest it
daily, charging on giant breakers
that trample all before it; pounding
civilization into a gritty powder
that brings the shore back to its primeval
beginnings. A crab must have been
one of the first to crawl out on that beach,
and grab   and grab   and grab!
I see you now, hellfit for chowder, tearing
the flesh away from any poor thing that merges
with your path: your murderous armor, your claws,
made not for love, but for wars. You are
ourselves, you are my self-destruction. You are
the perfect machine, with machine-clad body and
no face. What creators create such
things? You have no saving grace, not even
to be sometimes human. My stomach retches
as I watch you: you are tearing it out of me.
You are the end of the human race.

PART II

PART II

CHERRY TREE AND SNOW

Your curves, birds
perch upon, one
balancing the other,
higher up.
Just a brush
of feathers,
a smudge,
of white, or black.
Behind,
the snow sits.
Behind that, forest.
A quiet background
to your balance.
You curve,
and gently up,
and down,
in fountains,
the birds alight
on you,
and perch,
and sing.

CHERRY TREE AND ICE

The ice
transcends you!
How is it possible?

You wept in winter,
bare brown fountains
pouring toward the earth.
Now suddenly
they catch
in ice,
and you cascade in chime.

Who can believe your glitter?
Your gleam in greyness,
Your fire in sun?

You sparkle life!
Transfixed,
you catch in song.
You sing,
(then weep),
in sun.

MUSIC

How many musics   wend
   in wails   down   my waters,
railing   in   moving   space
   outcries   beyond
                                    time
                    and

                    place,   downspouts
after   rains,   mists
                            rising

                    or

                    after
suns,   for ears
                    that
                    hear:
   all in a   wave's   gong,   swirl
in   a   stream's   rush   like   the
   of a thrush,   like   gull's
                    the   a
                    whirl   of

                    cry,
waterbeads   ascending   back   to   the   sky
   in a   wet   whistle
   made   from a   grass-
                    blade
or   a   bamboo   rush   in   a   pond;

            a   memory   of   fond   rippless   quiet,
      or   a   rash   burst   of   heart
foaming   in   echoes   of   charge
            and   retreat   upon

                        the shore's

pangs,   of cymbals
                        with the bangs
      reverberating   in
                        the
                        heart-
                        space   of a life-
      time,
            in the   sound-   of a wind-
                        space

                        chime

      beside   the   airstrummed   lake.

She came into the sun
He entered her solitude
What was, was never
What could be, would never
be explained

The sun surrounded them
His touch was of the lily
The sand stretched into the sea
The sea moved onto the ground

The voices of the gulls caught fire
The sky merged with the sea
What was, was never
What could be, would never
be explained

The sun entered his thigh
She came out of his solitude
The solitude burst into flame
The sand burned onto flesh

The sea united with the sky
The lily was her breast
The gulls entered the air
The sand touched the sea

What was, was never
What could be, would never
be explained
The sand grew into the sea
The sea dissolved into land

The sky drank up the waves
The gulls shrieked into fire
They entered out of solitude
She came into the sun

What was, was never
What could be, would never be
The sand stretched wide around
The sun spilled into the sea

I lie with you
sunlit in meadows,
haysweet in grass,

the salamander sun
fusing us
like baked insects
to the clay-hard earth
below,

I rise with you,
filtering in rays
between laces of leaves
pendulously stirring
in our breaths
amid the trees,

man and lass,
laid out here
on display

    to the eyelidless sun

and the raucous jets, fun-
ny to observe our nakedness in

      the day, yet
      airy it is,
      and wet,

      and above we float

eternally

      between the hanging arches
        of the willow

and the weeping cherry,

meeting,
yet forever swaying separate,

leaves floating
                deciduous shadows
on our house walls
and our hearts,
                    bees
and cats   gnats and crickets
swarming us in this garden,
like fountains
showering the sun:

It is the hour.
"C'est l'heure!"

But we stretch out like the cat
in duplicate,
soak sun again,
keep time from moving forward
(nothing stirring now in our bower),

rewind our ticking,
become stillness in motion
like the hummingbird,
whirring,
beak to the flower

our noses filling us
with that rich-earth smell,

                    that warm decay
in the hay
        rising   into the leaf-sprayed air

You
breathe

in
waves

in the
tides

we
harvest

the
waters

the
seed

of
wonder

we
never

in
waves

in
sighs

in
days

we
soon

we
read

with
me

we
gather

of
nine-times

what
we

break
in-

gets
carried

and
its

know
the

we
breathe

we
gather

that
grow

will
ride

the
future's

in
waves,

seeds,

days,

feed;

side,

high,

shape,

why;

in
sighs,

love,

too
wide,

above;

cup,

we
sup

if
tears

then
love

and
weed

and
cares

will
know

and
cry,

spoil
love,

the
why.

SONGS FOR JEREMY

There was no emptiness at first,
but what had seemed complete
now grew so full that I could tell
there was no greater fullness.
In my own deep well
an invisibly small cell was suddenly
growing.
Could I have known the love that made you
would soon be overreached
by two loves stretching out to you?
You eased my belly out so gently,
I thought all women round like that,
and in my seasick shape,
my husband found anemones of light
and hulls burgeoning with treasure.
The day you came
I thought I felt an insistent,
urgent pressing;
and then the waters broke,
and waves and tides
carried you imperfectly ashore.

What made you tumble down so fast?
(They used to chide me for my slowness.)
You made everybody run to save you,
you were so out of breath.
Your father hardly breathed
the whole long time they handled us.
I pushed you down
till they could see you to reach up,
and with their one mute tug,
you came out swimming,
those perfect, narrow hips
leading to your legs' hard kicking.
Then, for that hot miraculous second,

they placed you
burning from the womb,
alert upon my belly.
We made you perfect till your ankles.
Was it your rash impetuousness
that made you rush out so fast,
you forgot to catch a breath
or straighten your feet?

Some people call the hospital sterile.
I think it is the mothers who are so.
How can they feed their young
from rubber nipples and glass hoses?
They brought you to me,
curled up like a rose,
your hands the first unfolded petals
resting on your snug blanket.
I received you,
and held you warm against my breast.
Your lips responded then.
They were your second petals,
and they fluttered sweetly around my flesh.
Even before the milk came in,
you, hungry for life,
knew about sucking.
All creation flowed in you.
I found you rich for touching.
We were entrusted with a life.

It was a miracle how love could flow.
No jealousy warped the rafters
of your father's house.
My breasts, once only for his touch,
were given wholly now to you.
He did not mind the loss;
he found much more
in watching your sweet lips enclosed in them,
and in the radiance of my face.
It pleased him that I had not grown

too civilized. You grew from mother's milk.
We thought you'd grow secure
from that warm intertwining.
Sometimes at night
I'd nurse you in your room
to keep your father sleeping.
Sometimes I'd creep with you
into his bed, and nurse your bright eyes
in his silence,
to keep from being lonely.
Sometimes he'd say from his light sleep
in early morning, nurse him here
so I can hold him too,
and then reach out his arm
until we intertwined.
Love flowed in our house.
We thought you'd grow
from our warm intertwining.

And suddenly you hover over us
with your awakening half-smile
reminding us of your too quick returning.
You were only just beginning to know
that love could be responded to.
You were no more than a ripple,
a blur upon water in time and space.
Should we smile back at your
shy fleeting? At that inner smile
that spread with such uncertainty
over your unpracticed face?
Or should we cry that those bright eyes
will never more nurse so intently
in the mother night's sweet-sucking stillness.
Why were you looking so hard at the white ceiling
that last night?

We were entrusted with a life.
It spilled through our fingers.
I shrink back in place,
and there is no trace of you.

FOG

See   the   dying
                               loved   back
                               ones

                  intothemist,

                      the
                      clear
                      warm
                      visions

                  blurringintothesoftwetgreys;

the   seawet   familiar   sticks
                             hand   shapes   and
                         stretching   and   shacks
                         out   fondnesses,   and
                         to   wicks
                         feel

finds   only   feathers   and   furs

        asthefogmovesinthickly,

                                   finds   shrouds

    and   dampened   sails   unfurled,   finds

weeping   memories   around   masts   that   slip

        away,

in   our   foghorn   failures;   sees

lifewarm
links   turned   into

phantoms in the breeze: mothers, fathers, friends,

chil-   lovers,   dren

all

lost   at   sea

in   the   fog,

so   fra-   gi-   ly

fa-   ding....

in   our   grey   daze,

did   we   ever   know   any

of   them?   Are   there

any   traces

of all those warm lost faces?

Yes,

Night   shines   lakes;
even   on
                black   though   shadows
                            shore-   weigh

       in   the   there   light
                       sun's   still   is
                       long
                       sleep,

dropped   to   awake
                from   moon-
                stars,   shimmers

       our   sleeping: even   on
                                  last   catch
                                  breaths   stars,

                   in   loved   though
                   hearts   of   ones,   far   they
                                                  mime

you,   at   shine
       in   night
       memory's   even   you   upon
                wakes;   still
                                                       lakes.

                fresh

You   dew   after   shimmering
                           a
                           dark
                           sleep,   on the tips
                                                             of grass!

warm   with   the
                            rising   your lips;
                            sun,

so   fair   and   your
                            fresh   face,

as   smooth   as   glass.

You,   our   morning   our   resurgence,
                            wetness,   middle-aged

                            our   seed
                                    refined,

           rising   over

a   wing   water,

                           God's

               airy   trace,

this   fragile   lass,

               our   daughter.

Falling
into the well
of your eye,
I flounder
in its spaces,
child
of my dark reaches,
like a novice swimmer
flailing in a crest of sea
that she can better
fathom
at rest,
my heartwheels
spilling shiny
in your depths
as you suck me
with a look
down to the tides
inside you,

playing our game
of eye to eye,
so close,
we really do flow
one into the other,
and neither
moon nor stars
light up my nights
the way the rays
of your eye
shoot light
within me.

CHILDREN

From my place in the dunes
they are separated
by three pieces of beach grass

They go to touch the waves in threes
like three grasshoppers
springing from three grassblades

They don't know
their scale has diminished
with my line of vision

Water flutters around their feet
like butterflies;
they bend over the water from the wind

The waves begin their long roll in
in threes
sun moon and earth align for high tide

The voices of children
spray above the moon force,
squeaking terns proclaiming silver fish

The children think they are brave
reinventing
the roar of the sea

Three hairs of grass
challenge
their magnitude

The boats move
towards each other
like two ants,
touch, and move on

flow horizontally
as their shadows
flow downwards

speaking
two languages
at dusk

swansong
willowsong

motion forwards
and
motion downwards

progressing
nowhere
but through
a beautiful
process

like the extension
of wings,
or the point in space
towards which
the dancer leaps,

and the people in the boat,
floating upside down

ripple

in the same undulation
as the willow

blur

in the same
breath of air
that disturbs
the surface tension

vibrate

and

disappear ....

Two people
in a boat
on the edge
of the universe,
two people
in an incan-
descence of water,
in an infinite
shine
in a wet nothingness,
two people
in a boat
on a watery radiance,
two people
over silent shadows
under two people
in a boat
poised for fishing,
two people
in a landscape
melting into water
rising into light
two
in
a
boat
with a long rod,
two, two
with
oars
poised
over
water
two people
on a grey day
in a green quiet
in a liquid lake
on a wet stillness
in an infinite peace
in two worlds
unseparated

AUREOLES

Monet caught the shine around the waterlily
until the form blew up into sheer light,
and the waterlily fragmented
into essence

Turner fled this world,
finding ropes of light
swinging between sky and sea,
blew his mind
with the light flashes
until he merged with them
into the swirling energy
of pure being

Vermeer haloed porcelain,
pearls, gold; even
milk, tiles and spinets,
painted women waiting
with shining porcelain faces
listening to the tides
in their wombs or the messages
written by distant lovers . . .
lit these up by the shaft
of light coming in
through an open door or window;
traveled that path
to the unspeakable light

And Wyeth blew the shimmer of light
through transparent curtains

catching the wind,
just as the shining grasses of his fields
caught the wind,
windows always looking out
towards the bright outside,
like the glassy faraway eyes
of Christina . . . .
found translucency
his essence

Blake spoke as he painted,
the light reaching him from above
but appearing as the glow of innocence,
the white incandescence
of the lamb as Christ,
the child as halo
sitting above the shoulders of man:
found that was essence

And I,
having eyes
but no brush,
lacking the radiation of color
yet knowing no religion but light,
follow all shiny things
to the surface
where the light strikes,
to the point of the ray
booming out like a laser beam,
paint poems of light
to that space
that blazes from beyond or above . . . .

And I too become essence

BOY WITH A CRAB, WELLFLEET BAY

Your legs grow upwards
from the water
like seagull posts
as you bend over the giant crab
you hold immobile by its tail.
Nothing else disturbs
the blinding openness of the sea,
not even the sky
which loses its line of demarcation
in the noonday shattering of light.
Everything merges in the shine
of the vast open mirror.
Waves have not yet unfolded in a pulse

Your eyes move out of time
as you measure the strangeness
of this new, encased sea shape
caught inside the circle of your pail.
My eyes move out of time
as I measure you
against the open bowl of the sea.
We stare in a resonance of light:
the sea rises silently
We pass from one state to another,
mutating like nuclei

The horseshoe crab lies low
in his pail under water.
Your breath passes over him
like your shadow moving

over rounded stones.
A sail appears somewhere
beneath the lost edges
of the sea and sky
Sun vibrates
through all our solid shapes
as though we were nothing but glass,
and we glow like kites
released into air

And is the light of the sea
any different from the light
of the field, and is the horizon
we step over by daybreak different
from the horizon we transcend
by nightfall, or the waving of grasses
in the wind less than the wind-blown wave?

And reaching this field from the ocean,
the same sun that was sinking
into the sea is falling into the hay,
the moon that lit the surf silver,
silvers the foam of Queen Anne's lace,
white gulls reverse to black crows,
cawing the same absurd story of the food
hunt, silver fish in the mouth
turn to golden corn bits

And the farmer of fish on the ocean
hauls the corn in from the field,
the lining up of ships at dusk
becomes the procession of animals
to the barn, the day's end lowers
the boom of the sun as the moon
rises over the stable

And is the light of the sea
any different from the light
of the field, and is the horizon
where tractors disappear to a point
any different from the point where
ships fall into the abyss, and is
the surrender of grasses to the wind
less than the moon ordering the waves?

Mr. Batdorf   lies there   sleeping,
lies there   sleeping,   Mr. Batdorf,
sleeping   there,   lies   Mr. Bat-
dorf   in   the   white   house   near
the cornfields;   growing   golden
in the fall-struck   is the   corn-high
tassled lovely   like cathedrals   in
the skylight,   with the sun   irradiating
through the stalks   in the   which way
that they bend,   in the   what way that
they blow,

                               with the corn still
                               all unshucked   in their whisper-
ings and scrapings,   they are wait-
ing   to   be   cut,   Mr. Batdorf
is not waking   nor the night high
after that,   with the full moon

                               shining stark
on the barn,   red and square,

                               squat and solid
it is there   in the waiting
like a still life   exposed,   with no
                                   shadow,
waiting there   for the corn
not to come,   for the pigs, not
to eat,   for the cats

                               not to scrap,

for the wife,   not to unite,

for the rains
not to fall,

                                                      Mr. Bat-dorf
not to rev   up the schoolbus
the next morning,   not to warm up
the laughters   of children   in the dawn
near the cornfields,

                                                      with the val-leys
                                                      lying fallow,

and the fall full of
the gorgeousness   and
of dying,   the
                              falling
                              leaves
                              all floating   and the night before,
                              down the
                              streams,   the red barn

                                                  lying moon-struck

                                                  and the weeks before

                  the sun-translucent grasses

                  luminescently all waving

as the children   all biked by,   Mr. Bat-field
was dying   in the dorf   by the sky

                  and the corn was waiting

to be shucked   and still is

                  and the children still ask   why

77

RAIN FOREST WITH CHILDREN

1

Your hands stare
out of the roots of trees,
lichen-white,
filaments of spring beauties
attaching themselves to bark,
grasping leaf mold and moulding logs,
mushrooming out of the darknesses of woods,
out of the wetness you bring
in your spring age.

2

Your eyes surprise me
from the forest's cavities,
playing like gnomes
in the hollows,
hiding, to seek;
seeking, to wind around
every nurse log and boulder
with the wild growth
of your youth,
laughing away the dark,
laughing away my age.

3

I wind on you like tears,
my slow descent back to roots
decaying the forest;
you asking me,
"will you cry again",
and I realize,
you only knew dew
till you found me
wet under my dark glasses.

4

How many of you now
spring out of trees,
dripping moss wigs
down to your shoulders?
You green me again,
spring me
from my rolled snail shape,
till I surge through earth
and unroll into fern.
I burst you children forth,
in threes,
and now you give life back,
threefold,
entwining my worst and my best
with the logs you multiply from.

5

Mushrooms,
wood beauties,
moss fairies,
carrying light on your shoulders,
dancing through hanging moss
like rays,
growing over me
with your roots searching water
(nurse log to your gay colonnade)
decay absolves my weight
and my tears nourish you,
grateful for your wetness.

6

On the edges of your elbows,
they sin away the trees,
hacking them flat
into forests of dead roots and limbs,
like bayonets entering villages of children.
The roots knife up in agony,
the wooden stumps unburied
till weather will wash their sores downstream
and eons spill them into oceans.
How soon the machines
chew into us all,
devouring us out of the soil.
We trumpet
from the farthest corner
of the wilds,
our feathers lashing into dust,
fed by the underground.
We roam the last plains of the west
until they zoo us into memory.
When will the sapling
child us back again?

Maturity   you chariot race

                   in the throes of time,

                                          you

Surfing   over the wave's shoulder,

   Unafraid,   sure,   and

Calling   the full brunt of your bolder power

                          in

Waters   that cannot scare you, although in

                   other years, in other hours, you

                   would not

Dare   to squander risk, to have failure

   Yanked   from under you.

Now   you don't

   Care   if the world

Crashes   down over your head;

                     the years

Behind   you needed, to prepare, and the years

   Ahead   suffice to

Gather   yourself together again, all the

   Broken   pieces, in one more valiant

Attempt   before you

   Die.   The wave

Ascends   again, about to crash in

   Fullness   or

Despair

LOVERS IN THE WATER

The lovers float there
in a confluence of kisses,
their bodies hovering
on an undulation of bliss,
every seam having floated away
into their soft fabric without edges,
every touch of their skin, a weightless
space trip, slippery wet, without friction;
they hang there by their lips,
their limbs fluttering out and in
like a blur of gull's wings,
everything hard dissolved
in their floating womb of water,
in their beginnings and endings;
and their wet kisses
are the suspension of time,
and their wet kisses
are the suspension of space,
and their wet kisses
are the coming together
of the universe

If I face the breakers head on,
if I strike the giant
at the midpoint,
if I combat it
when its full force
can drag me under
in the weakness of
middle age,
then I am a fool,
and certainly no hero

But if I head down
the long beach,
parallel to the waves,
after the fall of the breaker,
and the giant
is rattling its foamy tail
up and down the flat shore
and if it laps up and over
and around my feet,
then swishes back to the sea
in unexpected, clashing patterns,
motioning me playfully
to come to the combat,

And if the excitement
of the game of challenge
sucks me into the waves,
and the froth of action
whips me out of complacency,
then I stop being a fool,
though I am also no hero

So what am I, then,
woman, at midpoint,
having two faces
and two hearts,
    six hands,
    three feet,
    five surfaces like pillows,
    a body filled with fluids,
    veins throbbing
    under a mummy-thin skin,
    and infinite endurance
to walk in all directions
at the same time, with claws
hanging out of my shell

So what am I, then,
being raped
        abused
        loved
        ignored
        hungered after
        beaten
and discarded,
especially when
the fluids dry up
and the flesh sags,
or when I raise my voice
in protest

I also have such things as
an iron backbone
and an iron pelvis,
a skin responding to the flutter
of butterflies,
and a body pitted with holes
(through which I spill your lust)

And I love,
yearn after,
despise,
admire,
adore,
win,
lose,
barter my soul for protection,
chafe wildly in my apron strings,
burn them to seize greatness,
then flee to my house
when I see
the world is burning

And sometimes
I can
hate my body,
desire my body,
close tighter than a clam,
open wider than a waterlily,
seek warmth like a baby,
practice prostitution
three times a week,
remain innocence inviolate,
display my wares on the street
or hide them in tunics fluted
like Greek temples,
run sandalfooted,
touching the earth,
force my feet
to the pinched contours
of pigeon tracks,
dance like Theodora
in my living room
when no one is looking,
wear flowing robes one day
and the next day pants

I also pit the egos of children
against the egos of fathers,
come last instead of first,
resent mothers-in-law
who swallow their sons,
bend under the scorn of fathers
who shrink their daughters,
squirm under the warm, fat
bosoms of mothers,
realize that friends don't last
as long as relatives,
wish living together
were as simple as romance,
would rather be a mistress
than a wife,
splinter into four fragments
from the four bruised egos
that fight over my love

We struggle on the snow
The house nearby is a box
that holds us together
If somebody were to set a match to it
we would be released
I remember looking once
through the double-paned glass door
to the shadows moving
over the snow's surface
Shapes undulated and changed
The snow slid into white canvasses
(The snow, quiet as rabbit tracks
left as shadows during the night)
Black and white juncos spiraled down
from the weeping cherry tree
like cherry petals, snow dropping
off their wings, in falling notes.
I remember later trying to carve
the snow shapes
into white plaster,
trying to hold onto that calmness
of shadows
moving over an endless expanse
of whiteness
The double-paned glass door
held me to the inside
and to the outside
Now, this constant struggle with you,
like Laocoon with his snakes,
wrestling to be one
as the snow falls over our sheets

It is Monday
I take out
the garbage
It is growing every day
like a bubbling-over cauldron
I stuff it down stamp on it
run and get help to drag it
to the dump where seagulls swarm,
they having caught on to the fact
that there are more things there
than in the sea,
and as they fight over our remains,
they leave white feathers behind,
among other discarded things,
both beautiful and ugly,
such as dry flowers from graves
springs coiling up from old mattresses
grass clippings and wondrous other trash
the color of dried blood

And now, rose petals
scattered
above the garbage heap,
petals I saw today
floating by the shore
of our secluded lake,
floating
beside your half-submerged boat.
And I ask myself,
what is this age
but drowned petals,
drowned people,
loving in moored boats
that slowly sink in the waste
of polluted lakes, rotting timbers
of time, splitting from exploded
dreams and broken molecules

What are they doing
scattered about in droplets
over the jagged cans and
the putrefying flesh of the dump,
when before they were floating there?

Only the geese from the lake shore
can say, only their honking
dismay as they rush from the wars
of the waters that stop up
with the waste of this age;

and the drowned eyes of turtles,
of lovers unmoored, will rise
to the top, surveying
the killings and drownings,
the poisonings that cut the moorings

adrift and raise the bloated heads
of fowl and fish in the rift
made by people toward the lake;
and the bloated eyes will rage
and the bloated heads will shake.

And the drummer's drumming
on an inner tube's skin
will carry the rage
into the spastic body politic
before the stage is set
for a one-last-time dumping
of our age's rusting cars
and cans and wild-weird broken
flesh, yes, and broken chromosomes
and yes cockeyed atoms, yes
and yes yes, petals, petals
of roses, into the dinosaur-
flushing, into the atom-
degenerating bloody lake.

But Hell is also a charred car
outside New Jersey,
is being caught on the
Jersey Pike in a 4-lane fit
of thundering trucks
pounding past your ears
at 65mph, the market gardeners'
highway sealing you, in steaming tar,
from dewish morning leaves
and sun-translucent grass
in radiant seed, nowhere possible
in the stinks and smogs of oil tanks
and chimneys (do you remember
those dawn-swirled fogs from the sea
and birds curling skywards?) hot, God,
how he forgot what civilization could come to
on a stench-filled day, the trenches
of dirty towns along the highways
breathing in the rot; rejuvenation, creation,
never seeming more dim. Whatever sins
we make are hardly worthy
of this perpetual hell, but if
I picture it happening for infinity,
without a single foot on the brake,
it compares well with Dachau,
Bergen-Belsen, Dante's Inferno
(not 9 circles, just 5 senses):
though limbs aren't maimed,
and we are not quickly gassed
out of existence, our fingernails of eyes
have burning visions seared to them,
the ears are twisted round
and round till hanging loose
from maiming decibals of rock and roll and tire shrieks,
the sense that knew the rose is rubbed
incessantly in hot manures of taste,
the tongue is parched from countless burgers
snatched from cinder-covered picnics on

hell's balconies (from even 30 miles out,
the eyes begin to smart); the wave's thrust,
the tree-tall vision tarred away much like Pompei
in lavaspills of volcanic ash; the vision of
the Bay of Naples just a chariot ride away.
We are an ash can culture,
a corroded art of car heaps, a junk-
yard of the soul, a Welsh chorus of the steam-
roller, a vulture shrieking in the concrete streets.
We are the five senses of Hell.
We are life without water.

The boat
glides into twilight,
a dragonfly
fluttering wingoars

Silver ripples of breath
slide along
the lake's mirror surface

We enter silence!
ourselves reflected
on the underside of shadow

The willow
hangs
its long drapes
to the black bottom
of consciousness

Whatever exists
extends itself further

We wing through
unchartered spaces
that have no surface
for the planting of flags

The only reality
that
moves

is the boat

carrying
two men
on its frail
back

Your old boat, father,
sinking all these years

Your old boat,
lying in the algae,
encrusted with moss,

weeds growing up the cracks
faster than firecrackers!

Angled in green water
like a phone
half-off its hook

buzzing with insects
swimming
in the split-seam openings
of its sides

Your old boat
sinking all these years

A last turtle
of the lake
grasps a flake of paint
with one claw,
hard relic of antediluvian
wilderness;
a green bullfrog
hides
in a sunken corner
of the bow,

gold eyes lighting its caverns,
jade Buddha
in a golden temple

Suddenly,
this year,
at the slant of willows,
your boat devours water
as though thirsting
for the dark bottom
that reveals the whiteness
of the waterlily

Oh gold eyes in an old body,
hard shell enduring
as a giant tortoise,
how long can you encrust life
onto a failing boat,
like a ship
battered with barnacles

Your old boat tilts
like a knight ending battle,
and as it sinks,
I see you sitting at the bow,
thrusting your lance cantankerously
at frogs, turtles, weeds, algae,
everything invading your armoured domain,
as the water rises up around you

And now I too
wear the obstacles of age
like a death mask,
cheeks hanging like toads
over murdered ponds.
The rays bend
trying to join
the blurred sights of my eyes;
they have seen too much rage
hammering down as need
on the poor and defeated,
sabotaging the great
and the innocent,
exploding wisdom
into chaos.
You may wander
on the gullies
of my face,
trying to trace their history
with this or that.
You will find
only the mystery of surface.
You cannot touch
the volcanos of my living,
pitting the earthen crust
that fronts me,
raising it
into mountains and valleys
according to the tremors
of my heart.

My waters dry up,
yet see me, drowning,
in the spawning of young
salmon!
Parched under my
skinshade, like
flaked parchment, hear
my wet whistle
dying daily away
in the trammel of thick
hordes fighting the
moving stream; O,
what upstarts and divergencies
clamoring against the water's direction
and drowning the old guys
in a welter of sperm,
crowding us into a thicket
of old age, a withering sickness
that burns our memories
to oblivion and turns
our yellowing thoughts
into mill dust, lost
in the stream of forward motion.
I am an aged scroll buried
in a wet cave,
a fading thought
floating out to the seas
at the end of the streams
where all streams flow

And I dream my death
as man, not as woman,
for I go forwards
as well as backwards,
and I have had to don
the shells of man
even as women are now
shedding them,
but my body
will catch up to me
in the next century,
when all bodies
may radiate light

Light   water,
is water   light

          and while   its
                          under-
                          side   draws
                          of
                          night

darkly
down,   anchoring   in its
                          human   black
                          roots   bottom,
                                                             that many

lightyears   of pain   serve

     to   send   the   refractions   up again

that   the   of
let   follow   dropped   the
us   jewels   sun:

          light   water
          water   light

two
facets

     making   luminous

                          both
                          day
                          and
                          night,

                    changing

all   imperfections,

                    whatever is   ragged,
                    scarred and   dull,
                    marred,   or dry,

like debris   around   the   shores   of   a   lake,

                    into a   into a
                    shining   mysterious
                    holiness,   radiance

                         lengthening

                         all flatness

                    towards
                    the
                    muddy
                    roots   twirling   the
                    and   world
                    depths,

into a myriad   crystal-   faceted

              shimmering   microcosms,

through   ripples   of   the   wind   and   the   boat's

                                        rocking,

                    diversities
                    in harmony

linked   and made
in patterns   luminous
                                   by
                                   light,

by   the   sun   glancing   off the
                                                waters,

the   blaring   daily   world   blurred

into   the   muted   tones   of   watercolors,

          the   of the   the long
          submerged   mind   stretching
          indistinct   of
          world   spirit

                              everything
                              joined

into   like
geometric   tones
claspings
and arches,   spread out   like
                                               in harmonies   broken
                                                                   chords,

                              like
                              Bells,

reverberating   in   the   ripples   of   sunken

                    cathedrals,

pealing,   yet
                                                            never
                                                            knowing

                    beginnings or endings,

the submerged   under   hidden
underside   the   in
of life   human   wet
                                       boat   symbols.

EPILOGUE

Nature, you weather me wrong.
It is not this driftwood shape
I would be, however mellow
the stained and pitted lines
beneath my eyes, or round,
the smooth curves of this body,
battered by your bent waves;
nor the sigh of this soft drape,
hung to the blowing of time.
No matter, the poems that exit
from my weathered form and sit
on somebody's table to bring light;
these storms that shape me
bring me too much night.
There must be other ways
to hone a knife to beauty,
and cut your image into sight.
Nature, you've weathered me long.
Here is your driftwood poem. Now,
turn fair, and weather me right.